Summary

Of

Factfulness:

Ten Reasons We're Wrong About the World--and Why Things Are Better Than You Think

By

Hans Rosling

With Anna Rosling Rönnlund

and Ola Rosling

DEDICATION

For everyone who loves reading and books.

Whenever you read a good book, somewhere in the world a door opens to allow in more light. —Vera Nazarian

Table of Contents

Attention: Our Free Gift To You

As a way to say "Thank You" for being a fan of our series, we have included a free gift for you.

To get your free gift, please visit:

Concise Reading Team

Disclaimer

Note to readers:

This is an unofficial summary & analysis of Hans Rosling's "Factfulness: Ten Reasons We're Wrong About the World--and Why Things Are Better Than You Think" designed to enrich your reading experience.

Summary of Factfulness

Introduction

Hans Rosling (who will be referred to as Rosling from hereon) presents the reader with a short 13-question multiple choice quiz at the beginning of the book. There are three options for each question. The questions cover general knowledge questions about global development, e.g. extreme poverty rates, population growth, and access to education. For example, question 1 asks for the percentage of girls who have finished primary school in the world's low income countries (A: 20%, B: 40%, C: 60%). There are also questions about species extinction and global warming. He then reveals that he had posed this same quiz to thousands of people across the world and that the results have been shockingly underwhelming. On average, someone with no knowledge that guesses the answer to each question should get about four questions rights. The average test-taker, however, only got two questions right. 15% of the 12,000 people (in 14 countries) that took the quiz in 2017 got every single question wrong.

At first, Rosling had assumed that most people were ignorant of the world's realities because the knowledge they acquired in high school was updated. He initially attempted to "update" the knowledge of his audience through the use of lecturers with clear data animation and better teaching tools. He eventually realized that the majority of his audience was still stuck in their old and pessimistic worldview even after being presented with the facts. Even students at elite universities and the influential attendees of the 2015 World Economic Forum were not devoid of an outdated worldview.

Rosling theorizes that the early conditions of humanity – which were filled with starvation, war, violence, natural and man-made disasters, and corruption – had encouraged an "overdramatic worldview." The media is partly to blame, but people also gravitate towards misperception on their own. The state of things is always becoming worse, with resources running out and income inequality widening. With this stressful mindset, it is easy to overlook the fact that the majority of the world's population lives in the middle of the income class, and that the global poverty rate has been halved. To avoid the common misconceptions and overdramatic mindset, he argues that we need to consciously embrace "factfulness". This involves the inculcation of a fact-based worldview and control of our dramatic instincts.

Chapter 1: The Gap Instinct

Here, Rosling explains that each chapter (ten altogether) will cover a commonly held "dramatic instinct". The first instinct is the gap instinct, which he defines as "that irresistible temptation we have to divide all kinds of things into two distinct and often conflicting groups, with an imagined gap — a huge chasm of injustice — in between." He cites the example of dividing the world into "developed and developing" countries, or "the West and the rest". The former is rich, the latter poor. By using data of child mortality rates and fertility rates, he demonstrates that this distinction was true in 1965. Today, most countries have migrated from the "developing box" to the "developed box". 85% of humanity now has few children (low fertility) and a low mortality rate. However, the worldview inside the minds of many Westerners has not caught up. The outdated perception of a world divided between the wealthy West and the impoverished "Third World" persists.

In truth, however, the majority of humans today live in middle income countries. Rosling presents a four-stage model of human development to replace the simplistic and misleading concept of "developed" and "developing countries" (this model was been adopted by the World Bank, but not the UN):

- Level 1 (1 billion people): $2 income per day, an agrarian lifestyle without access to healthcare, transportation, formal education, and modern medicine;

- Level 2 (3 billion people): $4 income per day, access to formal primary education, a bicycle, and a gas stove;

- Level 3 (2 billion people): $16 income per day, access to running water and electricity, a motorcycle, formal secondary education, and savings

- Level 4 (1 billion people): $64 income per day, access to tertiary education, a car, and the conveniences of a modern consumer lifestyle

Rosling points out that the majority of the world's population live in Level 2 and 3 conditions, but those in level 4 tend to assume that everyone else is living in conditions that are similar to Level 1. They thus underestimate the extent to which people in low-income countries can access to good nutrition, vaccination, primary education, clean water, and an average life expectancy of 62 years. The majority of the test-takers assumed that over 50 percent of the world's population are living in a low-oncome country – but the actual percentage was only 9 percent. The dichotomy in many people's heads is thus inaccurate, overdramatic, simplistic, and instinctive.

To control the gap instinct, Rosling asks us to compare averages and the range for particular data points. He notes that gaps may exist in rare instances such as apartheid, but such a stark separation is an abnormality. We tend to be drawn to extremes, but this causes us to overlook the significant middle section. To be factful, look out for the majority and be cautious when making comparisons between averages and extremes.

Chapter 2: The Negativity Instinct

As the chapter title indicates, the second mega misconception is the instinct to pay more attention to the negative than the positive. Rosling points out that there are causes for alarm: the Syrian war has reversed the reduction in the number of war fatalities since World War II; overfishing is rampant; and the number of endangered species has increased. There is also the prospect of global warming, rising sea levels, and the possibility of another financial disaster. When asked the question "Do you think the world is getting better, worse, or remaining the same?" Most people – across all the countries that participated – believed that the world was getting worse.

Rosling points out that it is more difficult to pay attention to all the small improvements in the world than to the negative aspects. Most people fail to appreciate the phenomenal progress that has been made in the past few decades. The proportion of the world population living in extreme poverty has nearly halved (only 10 percent of people knew this). In 1800, 85% of the world lived in this impoverish stage (Level 1). Today, only 9% of the world's population live in this state. Much of the progress has been made by India, China, and Latin America. A similarly optimistic trajectory can also be seen in the average life expectancy (31 years in 1800; 71 years today). Even in the poorest countries today (e.g. Afghanistan), the quality of life has been improved through basic modernization (e.g. the use of plastic bags to store food, plastic buckets to store water, and soap to kill germs). Despite perceptions of doom, gloom, and chaos, every country in the world has improved its life expectancy in the past two centuries.

Rosling then presents 32 graphs to demonstrate how 16 bad things are decreasing and 16 good things are increasing.

The bad things include:

- legal slavery,

- oil spills,

- HIV infections,

- the price of solar panels,

- children mortality,

- war mortality,

- the number of countries with the death penalty,

- the number of countries that allow leaded gasoline,

- the number of plane crash deaths,

- the share of child laborers,

- deaths from disaster,

- the number of nuclear arms,

- the number of countries with smallpox cases,

- the amount of smoke particles emitted,

- the amount of ozone depleting substances emitted,

- the share of people who are undernourished.

The good things include:

- the number of new movies,

- scholarly articles and new music recordings produced each year,

- the amount of land mass that is gazetted for protection,

- the number of countries with female voters,

- harvest yields, the adult literacy rate,

- the share of humanity living in democracy,

- child cancer survival,

- the share of girls in primary school,

- the number of monitored species,

- and the share of the population with access to electricity,

- mobile phones,

- water,

- internet,

- immunization.

There are three key reasons for our tendency to pay more attention to the negative:

1. the way we misremember the past (by forgetting about prior brutalities and miseries);

2. selective reporting by activists and journalists (which prioritize the sensational and dramatic;

3. people also overlook the fact that not all human rights injustices in the past were reported, and the sentiment that things are not improving if they are still bad.

Today, the "surveillance of suffering" across the world is at its peak with the easy accessibility of phone cameras, videos, social media posts, and online articles. Ultimately, people *feel* that the world is getting worse even when the evidence suggests otherwise. There are many injustices that still exist today (e.g. plane crashes, climate change deniers, preventable child deaths, sexism, endangered species, male chauvinists, crazy dictators, toxic waste, and journalists in prison), but this does not negate the progress that has been made.

To reign in our negativity instinct, Rosling suggests the following measures:

- Keep two thoughts in your head when you see negative news: the world can be bad, but yet better than it was before; saying that "things are improving" does not mean that everything is fine.

- Anticipate bad news and negative stories (since this is more likely to reach us), while looking out for positive and gradual changes that may not be so evident.

- More bad news could be the result of more surveillance and not more suffering.

- Do not see history through a censored lens.

- Be thankful for the gains that your society has achieved.

Chapter 3: The Straight Line Instinct

The third misconception involves the straight line instinct, which assumes that things that increase (e.g. the world population, the number of Ebola victims) are increasing in a linear fashion, and that things which have been increasing will increase at the same rate in the future. For example, most people assume that the number of children in the world (2 billion today) will increase to 3 or 4 billion by 2100 (when UN statisticians predict that it will remain the same). The world population will continue to increase (at a slower rate, at the flattening out at 10-12 billion people), but this is because there will be more adults in the future. They know this because the fertility rate has dropped to below 2.5 today, and is projected to keep decreasing. As more women escape extreme poverty and gain access to education and contraception, they will be likelier to give birth to fewer children.

Rosling observes that people tend to rely on anecdotes (e.g. large families in Africa and Latin America or the avoidance of contraceptives in the Catholic world) to dispute the projection that the world's population will eventually stop increasing. He points to the data to reveal that the average family across the world includes only two children. It is the poorest 10 percent that has an average of five children. People tend to assume that helping poor children will result in an unsustainable population increase, without accounting for the fact that parents living in extreme poverty tend to have more children because of greater child mortality rates. When they have access to better conditions, they will invest in fewer children – regardless of culture, tradition, and religion. On the other hand, allowing extreme poverty to perpetuate will only produce a larger next generation.

To avoid the tendency to assume to think in straight lines (and understand that graphs come in curves of all shapes), you can take note of the following:

- Straight lines can be found when correlating income levels with (1) health; (2) amount of schooling; (3) bride age; (4) recreation.

- When income is correlated with basic necessities like primary education or vaccination, you can expect S-shaped curves (people will obtain them as soon as they can afford to).

- A downward slope (a slide) can be found for the correlation between income levels and fertility rates, as well as the cost of vaccinations.

- Humps can be found when graphing the correlation between income levels and phenomena like cavities, traffic deaths, and the number of children dying. With increasing access to cars and sweets alongside a lack of preventive public education, the middle income nations will suffer more from certain ailments.

- Doubling lines (where something is increasing exponentially) can be found when graphing income against travel distance, spending on vehicles and transport, and carbon dioxide emissions.

Chapter 4: The Fear Instinct

Rosling opens the chapter with an anecdote to illustrate how we cannot see things accurately when we are afraid.

He had once mistakenly assumed that World War III was occurring while treating a pilot who had been admitted to his emergency ward. In fact, the pilot had been muttering gibberish instead of Russian because his plane had crashed into icy water (during a routine flight, and not a military operation). He was not suffering from an epileptic seizure or bleeding to death – Rosling had been stepping on a color ampule in the life jacket and assumed that the red ink on the floor was the pilot's blood.

When we are overwhelmed by fear, we see what we are afraid of seeing – and pay no attention to the facts.

Since we tend to pay more attention to information that fits our dramatic instincts while ignoring information that does not, we end up with a distorted view of reality. Naturally, it is the unusual stories that make the headlines and captures everyone's attention. Humans tend to be most afraid of snakes, spiders, heights, and being trapped in small spaces. After that, they are most afraid of public speaking, needles, airplanes, mice, strangers, dogs, crowds, blood, darkness, fire, and drowning. Journalists and media institutions capitalize on these natural fears, leaving us with an image of a dangerous and deadly world – even though it has never been safer and less violent. When we see images and video clips of human suffering, we lose track of the big picture and become overwhelmed with sympathy, empathy, and the feeling that we need to do something to help.

Despite claiming much attention, our biggest fears are hardly the deadliest. Natural disasters (0.1 percent of all deaths), plane crashes (0.001 percent), murders (0.7 percent), nuclear leaks (0 percent), and terrorism (0.05 percent) are all responsible for less than

1 percent of deaths each year. Since the dawn of the environmental movement, the developed world has been plagued with fears of chemical contamination (chemophobia). Rosling argues that what is "frightening" and "dangerous" are two disparate entities. If we pay too much attention to perceived risks, we ignore the real risks that could actually harm us. We need to be aware that the most frightening things are not necessarily the most risky, and that risk depends on the level of danger and our level of exposure to it. Finally, be sure to make decisions only when the panic subsides and you regain a calm state of mind.

Chapter 5: The Size Instinct

To illustrate our common tendency to get things out of proportion, Rosling describes his harrowing experience as a young doctor in Mozambique in the early 1980s.

With limited medical infrastructure and staff, many of the children under his care died due to diarrhea, pneumonia, and malaria. These diseases were made more severe by malnourishment and anemia. At the time, Rosling had decided to allocate some scarce resources towards efforts to focus on preventive measures (organizing, supporting, and supervising basic community-based healthcare) as opposed to saving the children who were already dying. This was not an easy decision to make (he described it as "the cruel calculus of extreme poverty" and "an almost inhuman" choice), but he argued that it was actually more heartless to focus on the symptoms of the problem instead of the actual problem: "It would, I believed, be truly unethical to spend more resources in the hospital before the majority of the population—and the 98.7 percent of dying

23

children who never reached the hospital—had some form of basic health care." At the end of the day, it was more heartless and cruel to avoid focusing on how you could save as many lives as possible – even if it meant directing resources away from the dying child in front of you.

Rosling argues that we tend to misjudge the size of things because we often focus on single numbers or statistics. Journalists also often present their stories, news, and reportage as being more important than it actually is. When combined with our tendency towards negativity, this means that many people underestimate the amount of progress that has been made in the developing world (and the developed world, with regards to other issues like tolerance towards the LGBT community).

To keep our size instinct in check, we should do the following:

- Look out for the individual stories behind the statistics;

- Compare big numbers to get a better sense of scope (e.g. 4.2 million babies died in 2017, should be contextualized against the number in 1950: 14.4 million);

- Be alert to the 80/20 rule: it is often the case than a few items on a list are more important than all the others put together;

- Determine if there is the possibility of biased media coverage (e.g. deaths by animal attacks vs. deaths by everyday causes like domestic violence and "unsensational" diseases like tuberculosis);

- Divide the numbers to obtain the rates for a phenomenon (e.g. 4.2 million babies dying each year translates to an infant mortality rate of 3%; the news that India and China are the world's largest polluters makes sense given their large populations);

- If you live in a relatively safe country, take note of which global disasters are unlikely to affect you.

Chapter 6: The Generalization Instinct

This chapter is filled with anecdotes about how we tend to over-generalize and inaccurately group together things, or people, or countries that are actually very different. Rosling acknowledges that we tend to be more familiar with race and gender stereotyping and focuses his analysis on how people living in Level 4 conditions tend to over-generalize when it comes to the everyday realities of people living in Level 2 and Level 3 conditions:

- Even educated professionals underestimate the accessibility of vaccines to the world's children (80%).

- Sanitary pad manufacturers overlook the fact that women in Level 2 and Level 3 countries have a real need for their products and waste their time by marketing more niche pads (e.g. yoga pads) to their limited customer base in Level 4 countries.

- One of his Swedish medical students assumed that lift in India had motion sensors and nearly lost her leg in the process.

- While studying as a fourth-year medical student in Bangalore, Rosling himself assumed that his Indian classmates would be less academically prepared than he was.

To avoid over-generalizing and stereotyping, Rosling suggests that we do the following:

- Instead of thinking about "poor/developing" and "rich/developed" countries, think about how people with similar income levels in different countries can live very similar lives and how there can be large differences in living conditions within the same country.

- Take note that many of the images of everyday life that you see in the media will tend to be from Level 4 countries, since the most influential media institutions are based there.

- When you see the phrase "the majority", ask for a specific percentage as this could be anything from 51%-99% to gain a more nuanced understanding.

- Be careful when assuming that a certain practice is attributed to a culture/nation/religion instead of their income level.

- Avoid sweeping generalizations, e.g. Africa consists of 54 countries and 1 billion people but Westerners assume it is homogenous.

- Beware of exceptional examples, e.g. some chemicals are harmful while others are perfectly harmless.

- Instead of assuming that other people are not "normal", assume that you are the one who has lived a different reality so that you can better understand an unfamiliar context.

- Avoid generalizing from one group to another.

- If something appears strange or unusual, assume that there is a unique logic behind it and make inquiries before jumping to conclusions.

Chapter 7: The Destiny Instinct

The destiny instinct involves the idea that "innate characteristics determine the destinies of people, countries, religions, or cultures." It assumes that things have always been as they are and cannot change in the future. Instead of understanding that societies and cultures are fluid and dynamic, we tend to assume that they remain stagnant and cannot be altered even if there are significant efforts to change the status quo. Many of Rosling's examples revolve around the Western perception that Africa is and will always be a "basket case" and it can never attain the European standard of living. There are also a few examples about how people tend to falsely believe that the "Islamic world" is fundamentally different from the "Christian world." On the flip side, people living in Level 4 countries tend to overlook the fact that their grandparents were living in the same conditions of extreme poverty that the Level 1 countries today face.

Rosling notes that these perceptions are not inconsequential. When IMF forecasters underestimate the rate of economic growth in Level 2 and Level 3 countries, they prevent these countries from benefiting from foreign investment. Likewise, many companies in the "West" overlook the market opportunities that are taking shape in Africa and Asia as the middle-income consumer market there expands significantly. To be more perceptive of how things can change over time, we should do the following:

- Differentiate between slow change and no change: even small changes (e.g. 1% per year) can translate to a major difference years down the line.

- Be conscientious about updating your knowledge: what you learn in the social sciences becomes irrelevant very quickly as technology, countries, societies, cultures, and religions are constantly changing.

- Talk to your parents and grandparents to get a better sense of how the conditions around you have changed over time.

- Actively look out for examples of cultural change.

- Try to be more aware of how you might be projecting the past into the future.

Chapter 8: The Single Perspective Instinct

It is easier to conceive of the world in simple terms, and this is what most people tend to do. We often think that all problems have a single cause, or that all problems have a single solution. In reality, of course, this is often far from the truth. The examples that Rosling relies on in this chapter mostly draw contrasts between the state of affairs in Cuba (a single minded communist country) and the United States (a single minded capitalist country). Americans tend to assume that the free market can solve all their problems, while government intervention is responsible for all their woes. Cubans, on the other hand, believe that central planning should be sufficient by itself in solving all the country's challenges.

To adopt a more multi-faceted and accurate view of the world, we should do the following:

- Do not adopt a blanket for/against stance against any particular idea.

- Test your favorite ideas for weaknesses.

- Note that experts and activists are often only knowledgeable within their very specific field, but they will often presume themselves to be experts on domains outside of their immediate expertise.

- Note that activists often exaggerate the problems that they have dedicated themselves to.

- Numbers and statistics are useful, but some aspects of reality cannot be measured in numbers alone (or at all). This includes cultural, historical, ideological and sociological nuances and particularities.

- Avoid confirmation bias by engaging with people who disagree with you.

- Be aware of the limitations of your own knowledge and expertise.

- Be wary of simple ideas and simple solutions.

Chapter 9: The Blame Instinct

When something bad happens, the blame instinct often kicks in – compelling us to look for a simple reason (or a single person or entity) responsible.

Rosling notes that it is easier to attribute negative outcomes to "bad individual with bad intentions". If we do not believe that some individuals had the power and agency to shape events, the world becomes more unpredictable, confusing, and frightening. On the flip side, we are also ready to give the credit to a particular individual or a simple case even though the reality of the situation is often more complicated. Our readiness to find people to blame or credit often prevents us from solving the problem. It also distracts from the more complex reality at hand.

Rosling then explains how the three entities we often blame – businessmen, journalists, and foreigners – are often only a part of the problem. Businessmen can be innovative, inventive, and willing to take risks to obtain cheaper and better solutions. Journalists do have their own distorted worldview and a tendency towards over-dramatizing information, but why should we assume that the sum of all the stories they present will amount to a representative view of the world? And when it comes to foreigners, it is easier to blame them (e.g. for rising global emissions) instead of acknowledging our own complicity in the problem.

To be more aware of how scapegoats are often used to divert your attention, you should do the following:

- Look for multiple causes and systemic problems instead of finding a villain.

- If something good happens, think of how systems, institutions, and technology may have played a more important role than the individual.

Chapter 10: The Urgency Instinct

This chapter includes examples of how government reactions to public health crises in Mozambique and the Democratic Republic of Congo led to severe unintended consequences. When a mayor decided to set up a roadblock to contain a possibly infectious disease, villagers who were intending to travel to the city to sell their goods decided to go there by hiring fishermen instead. When the boats capsized, they all drowned. In Congo, a roadblock led to a food shortage and caused food poisoning (when the people could not wait for cassava roots to be processed and ate them immediately).

These real life examples illustrate how we often make very bad decisions when we are under time pressure, afraid, and only thinking of worst-case scenarios. The urge to make a quick decision and act immediately prevents us from thinking analytically and carefully considering the data and evidence at hand. When there is both fear and urgency, the outcome is often drastic decisions that cause unpredictable side effects. This instinct may have been adaptive in the past (particularly in the savannah plains where humans first evolved), but it does not help us with the more complex, abstract, and long term challenges we face today.

Rosling points out that activists (and climate change activists in particular) often feel the need to exaggerate the problem at hand to create fear and compel action. He argues that this is not wise in the long run, since the future is always uncertain to some degree. Furthermore, presenting the worst-case scenario and most drastic estimates will ruin the reputations of scientists and activists – and cause them to be ignored. They should rely on systematic analysis, thought-through decisions, incremental actions, and careful evaluation.

The chapter concludes with a list of Rosling's major concerns (that we should worry about):

- **Global pandemic.** An airborne disease like flu is a greater threat than Ebola or HIV.

- **Financial collapse.** Economists have a bad track record in predicting it.

- **World war.** Without world peace, no sustainability goal can be achieved.

- **Climate change.** Global cooperation is needed to overcome this challenge.

- **Extreme poverty.** This leads to civil wars and additional poverty – a vicious cycle.

Chapter 11: Factfulness in Practice

The chapter begins with a story of how a courageous village woman in a poor village in the Democratic Republic of Congo saved Rosling's life. He had travelled there to collect blood samples for his research on konzo (an incurable paralytic disease). The villagers had threatened to kill him out of the fear instinct (by the needles, the blood, and the disease), the generalization instinct (Europeans were plunderers), the blame instinct (the evil doctor was here to steal their blood and sell it), and the urgency instinct (the doctor must be stopped immediately). He noted that her ability to convince her fellow researchers on the role that medical research (which involves drawing blood samples) plays in disease prevention revealed logic, critical thinking, and the ability to express her thoughts clearly and convincingly to persuade her fellow villagers. Here, Rosling explains how you can utilize Factfulness in your everyday life in the same manner:

- **Education.** Children should be taught about basic facts from all parts of the world (and these facts have to be updated as the world changes). They should be more aware about stereotypes and historical changes, and be taught humility and curiosity.

- **Business.** Many Western multinationals and financial institutions are trying to operate according to an ingrained, outdated, and distorted worldview. Global data is more available now, but it can be misinterpreted without global knowledge.

- **Journalism, Activism and Politics.** We should be aware that they will always try to engage our attention with dramatic stories and exciting narratives – the unusual over the commonplace. Instead of expecting media reform, you should consume the news more "factfully" – and realize its limitations.

- **In your organization or community.** Look out for ignorance in the people closest to you – they can surprise you with their eagerness to learn.

Background Information About

Factfulness

Hans Rosling, a Swedish Professor of International Health and global TED sensation, has described *Factfulness* as his "last battle" in his life-long mission to fight "devastating ignorance". Throughout his career, he discovered that teachers, investment bankers, Nobel laureates, and journalist were often systematically wrong when asked to answer simple questions about global trends (e.g. the percentage of the world's population that lives in poverty). With inspiring and compelling anecdotes and stories, the book *Factfulness* makes facts and statistics interesting. It focuses on the ten instincts that distort our worldview and prompt us to rely on stereotypes, unconscious and predictable biases, dramatic instincts, and emotions when thinking about the world. The book ultimately aims to empower you to react to future opportunities and challenges with a more fact-based mind-set. The book's title can be defined as "The stress-reducing habit of only carrying opinions for which you have strong supporting facts." Bill Gates has described it as "one of the most important books I've ever read[1]."

---

[1] http://time.com/5224618/bill-gates-hans-rosling-factfulness/

Background Information About Hans Rosling, Ola Rosling, and Anna Rosling Rönnlund

Factfulness was the final chapter in Hans Rosling's illustrious career as a professor of international health, a medical doctor with a global perspective, and a noted public educator (he passed away in 2017). He has served as an adviser to UNICEF and the WHO. He co-founded the Gapminder Foundation (which promotes global sustainable development through statistics and awareness-raising) and Médecins Sans Frontières. His TED talks have been viewed by over thirty-five million people across the world. In 2012, he was listed as one of TIME magazine's one hundred most influential people in the world for his "stunning renderings of the numbers that characterize the human condition[2]."

Ola Rosling and Anna Rosling Rönnlund are Rosling's son and daughter-in-law. They were both co-founders of the Gapminder Foundation, and have worked with Rosling's data visualizations and presentations over the decades. Ola has also served as the Gapminder Foundation's director from 2005-2007, and from 2007 to the present.

---

[2]

http://content.time.com/time/specials/packages/article/0,28804,2111975_211 1976_2112170,00.html

They invented and designed the innovative bubble chart tool known as Trendalyzer, which was acquired by Google in 2017. Ola now serves as the head of Google's Public Data Team, while Anna serves as its senior user-experience (UX) designer.

Cover Questions

1. What is the difference between an optimist and a "possibilist"?

2. How can our instinct to turn people into heroes impede progress?

3. Which is it more productive to organize populations by how they live instead of where they live?

4. Why is it important to look at the data *and* to spend time with people?

5. What did Rosling mean when he argued that things can be bad but better?

Trivia Questions About

Factfulness

1. Which billionaire and noted philanthropist reviewed the book on his personal blog?

2. When did Rosling start writing the book and why?

3. Who does Rosling credit for showing him "a world completely different from the one [he] learned about in school"?

4. What is the first personal anecdote that appears in the book?

5. Who were some of the groups of people that Rosling administered his Gapminder quiz to?

6. When and where did Rosling start his "lifelong battle against global misconceptions"?

Trivia Questions About

Hans Rosling

1. Why did Rosling master the art of sword-swallowing?

2. How did Rosling befriend Bill and Melinda Gates?

3. What nearly got Rosling killed in the Democratic Republic of Congo?

4. What is Rosling's advice to Western manufacturers of the sanitary pad?

5. How did Rosling challenge his Swedish students about their assumptions between the West and the Rest?

Discussion Questions

1. Why did Rosling invent the four income group framework of classifying humanity?

2. Why do people in the West tend to underestimate Africa's possibility for progress?

3. How did humans come to possess the overdramatic instinct?

4. Which of the 13 questions in the Gapminder Test has the lowest average score?

5. What are some of the 16 "terrible things" that are eventually disappearing?

6. How does the news environment today distort our view of the world?

7. What is the 80/20 rule?

8. Why does Rosling warn us to not censor history?

9. How does Rosling debunk the common perception that Muslims and Catholics will always have large families because of their religious beliefs?

10. How does Rosling qualify his belief that liberal democracy is "the best way to run a country"?

Thank You

We hope that you've enjoyed your reading experience.

Here at Concise Reading, we will always strive to deliver to you the highest quality guides.

We'd like to thank you for supporting us and reading until the very end.

Before you go, would you mind leaving us a review on Amazon?

It will mean a lot to us and help us continue to create high quality guides for you in the future.

Yours warmly,

Concise Reading Team

Made in the USA
San Bernardino, CA
13 July 2018